MW00637901

Destination: This Moment

Teena Merlan

hippo pub co

ISBN 978-1-7372330-1-5 (ebook)
ISBN 978-1-7372330-0-8 (hardcover)

Cover art and illustrations by Kaki Okumura
Edited by Jon Davis
Design by Alvaro Villanueva
Foreword by Ashley Sharp

Printed on 100% recycled paper by Bookmobile in the United States of America
First Edition: March 2022

Published by hippopubco
hippopubco.com

in loving memory of my father,
Art Merlan

contents

foreword

In 2018, I traveled to the high country of New Mexico along
the continental divide to practice mindfulness and rest into
the natural world for five weeks. Unquestionably, this period of
practice and nature bathing changed my life for the better in both
obvious and not-so-obvious ways. During that time, spurred on
by the clear seeing that mindfulness brings about, I decided to
pursue a long-held dream to live in a quieter way and offer the
practices of mindfulness, art, and healing in a remote, rural setting.

Fast forward through the process of quitting my work, selling my
house and leaving the urban area that I had called home for more
than 25 years, not to mention the emergence of a global pandemic.
Three years have passed, and I am now living at and running a
small retreat center in Northern California. The center is on 25
acres with an apple orchard, a redwood forest, and a year-round
creek filled with salmon. Even with the pandemic, people have
been visiting, practicing mindfulness and art, and absorbing the
fresh air and quiet.

This is how I met Teena. She came for a short retreat from her life and to practice mindfulness. At that time, little did I know how talented and creative she is. She spent a few days here leaving gifts, art, and love. It turns out she was also writing while here. Some months later, I was delighted to read and muse on her beautiful poetry with the stunning images of Kaki Okumura.

Whenever anyone practices mindfulness, there is the potentiality and power of both large and small change. Mindfulness is an ancient practice arising from the cultures and wisdom teachings of southeast Asia. More than two millennia ago, a man named Siddhartha Gautama (the Buddha) looked inward through meditation, named and then taught the life-changing practice of mindfulness.

People have written everything from scholarly tomes to verbose self-help books on mindfulness and straightforward wisdom. These writers endeavor to elucidate the deceptively simple and ever-deepening practice of mindfulness. Through her poetry, Teena has taken this ancient technique and made it easy to understand while highlighting the poignancy of the practice. This is no small feat. Mindfulness, when practiced with sincerity, brings wisdom — like the wisdom that Teena shares here with us.

It is a misunderstanding to think that the power of mindfulness is only available to those who meditate for hours. Mindfulness can be practiced on the meditation cushion but is never limited to the cushion. It can be as simple as taking a breath, paying attention while doing something ordinary like washing dishes, or absorbing art and words.

It is thrilling to know that you, the reader, have the opportunity to engage with your life through the poetry and art in this volume. Take your time as you read. Let the words settle and echo through your body, mind, and heart so that the reading and images themselves become a practice of paying attention. Savor the beauty that is here before you.

—*Ashley Sharp*

Inattention

This moment becomes
the next—in a blink, a breath—
without permission.

Breakneck Pace

We're lost in doing,
no spare moment to process—
not even to breathe.

Sight Unseen

Struggling wildly
inside our own minds and hearts.
How do we quiet?

Weather the Storm

Centered in your trunk,
you are not easily swayed.
Come whatever may.

Progress

Even when we fall,
we land in the valley fore.
We do not slide aft.

Mantras

What we tell ourselves
becomes our reality.
Use your words wisely.

Silence

Through empty stillness,
inside and out, we create
space to be ourselves.

You Are Home

Truer than ever,
you have no place else to go
so be where you are.

Journey

Life is a journey.
The destination is *this*
moment. Now *this* one.

Savor

Dishes, laundry, poop.
These moments comprise our lives.
Let us live them all.

You Are Here

Breathe in, breathe out. Ahhh—
pause within this found moment.
That's how you arrive.

Forthcoming

Finding only faults
is to speak in pure falsehoods.
Let us be honest.

Onward

The call from within
demands action—and courage.
You have all you need.

Crossroads

Feeling uncertain.
Deep breath. Clear eyes. Willing heart.
Take a leap of faith.

Rebirth

The great illusion
of beginning and ending—
truly, they are one.

Attention

> Each stone on the trail
> hides untold marvels beneath.
> Enjoy your travels.

Fleeting

With an open heart,
every moment is a chance
for infinite love.

Inward

Prickles, flutters, warmth.
Hidden beyond thinking mind,
your innate wisdom.

Growing Pains

> *Metamorphosis,*
> says the brave caterpillar,
> *demands sacrifice.*

Trust

Sit with what is here,
release what you expected.
This path *is* your path.

Abundance

Profound gratitude
in even the darkest hour—
thus, blessings arise.

Vast

Emerging anew,
the butterfly knows no bounds.
All is within reach.

Sovereignty

Now set yourself free
from the bonds that burden you.
Divine liberty.

Boundless Joy

And there—within you—
Unbound. Blinding. Beautiful.
Your heart is ablaze.

about the author

Teena Merlan has been writing in some form or another basically since she learned how. Her poetry has been published in small literary magazines across the country, her blogs and technical writing appear on various websites, and she is an avid fan of journaling. She was accidentally introduced to meditation during her senior year of high school and began a more formal sit practice and other mindfulness modalities around 2010, including yoga, daylongs, and silent meditation retreats. She has been practicing mindfulness, meditation, and Buddhism ever since and is constantly applying and deepening her practice in every facet of life.

about the illustrator

Kaki Okumura is a Japanese illustrator. Her work has been featured in publications like *Heated x Mark Bittman*, *the Beet*, *Yes! Magazine*, *S&P Magazine*, *Elemental*, and *Forge*. She is currently in New York, NY.

To discover more of her work, please visit www.kakikata.space.